50 Recipes for Protein Desserts for Weight Training:

Accelerate Muscle Mass Growth without Pills or Creatine Supplements

By

Joseph Correa

Certified Sports Nutritionist

COPYRIGHT

© 2016 Correa Media Group

All rights reserved

Reproduction or translation of any part of this work beyond that permitted by section 107 or 108 of the 1976 United States Copyright Act without the permission of the copyright owner is unlawful.

This publication is designed to provide accurate and authoritative information in regard to the subject matter covered. It is sold with the understanding that neither the author nor the publisher is engaged in rendering medical advice. If medical advice or assistance is needed, consult with a doctor. This book is considered a guide and should not be used in any way detrimental to your health. Consult with a physician before starting this nutritional plan to make sure it's right for you.

50 Recipes for Protein Desserts for Weight Training:

Accelerate Muscle Mass Growth without Pills or Creatine Supplements

By

Joseph Correa

Certified Sports Nutritionist

COPYRIGHT

© 2016 Correa Media Group

All rights reserved

Reproduction or translation of any part of this work beyond that permitted by section 107 or 108 of the 1976 United States Copyright Act without the permission of the copyright owner is unlawful.

This publication is designed to provide accurate and authoritative information in regard to the subject matter covered. It is sold with the understanding that neither the author nor the publisher is engaged in rendering medical advice. If medical advice or assistance is needed, consult with a doctor. This book is considered a guide and should not be used in any way detrimental to your health. Consult with a physician before starting this nutritional plan to make sure it's right for you.

ACKNOWLEDGEMENTS

The realization and success of this book could not have been possible without my family.

50 Recipes for Protein Desserts for Weight Training:

Accelerate Muscle Mass Growth without Pills or Creatine Supplements

By

Joseph Correa

Certified Sports Nutritionist

CONTENTS

Copyright

Acknowledgements

About The Author

Introduction

50 Recipes for Protein Desserts for Weight Training

Other Great Titles by This Author

ABOUT THE AUTHOR

As a certified sports nutritionist and professional athlete, I firmly believe that proper nutrition will help you reach your goals faster and effectively. My knowledge and experience has helped me live healthier throughout the years and which I have shared with family and friends. The more you know about eating and drinking healthier, the sooner you will want to change your life and eating habits.

Being successful in controlling your weight is important as it will improve all aspects of your life.

Nutrition is a key part in the process of getting in better shape and that's what this book is all about.

INTRODUCTION

50 Recipes for Protein Desserts for Weight Training: Accelerate Muscle Mass Growth without Pills or Creatine Supplements

This book will help you increase the amount of protein you consume per day to help increase muscle mass. These meals will help increase muscle in an organized manner by adding large healthy portions of protein to your diet. Being too busy to eat right can sometimes become a problem and that's why this book will save you time and help nourish your body to achieve the goals you want. Make sure you know what you're eating by preparing it yourself or having someone prepare it for you.

This book will help you to:

-Gain muscle fast naturally.

-Improve muscle recovery.

-Eat delicious food.

-Have more energy.

-Naturally accelerate Your Metabolism to build more muscle.

-Improve your digestive system.

Joseph Correa is a certified sports nutritionist and a professional athlete.

50 RECIPES FOR PROTEIN DESSERTS FOR WEIGHT TRAINING

1. Vegetarian high-protein quinoa pie

Ingredients:

Quinoa - 135 g in the dry state

Zucchini - 200 g finely chopped (3-4 mm cubes)

Carrots - 100 g finely chopped (3-4 mm cubes)

Liquid egg white - 200 g (about 6 eggs)

Whole-wheat flour - 40 g

Shallot (or normal onion) - 30 g

Garlic - 10 g

Farmer soft cheese - 125 g (you may use mozzarella or Cheddar, but low-fat)

Salt, pepper, spices to taste

Olive oil - 2-3 g (for pan coating)

Method of preparation:

1. Seethe the quinoa.

2. Put the casserole dish into the oven and heat it till 180 C. The casserole dish needs to be heated in order the baked pie to be golden brown on each side.

3. Cut the carrots and zucchini into small cubes; mince the onion and garlic.

4. Grate the cheese.

5. Work the egg albumen into a rich lather and add 100 g of grated cheese. The rest of the cheese (25 g) will be used for powdering the pie's surface.

6. Add the chopped vegetables, quinoa, salt pepper and dry spices to the eggs. Mix it thoroughly.

7. Stir it all together with the whole-wheat flour.

8. Pull out the hot casserole dish from the oven, oil it and pour the whole mixture pressing in boards in order to remove the holes. Powder the rest of the 25 g cheese on top.

9. Bake at 180 C 40 minutes exactly, depending on oven.

Nutrition per 1/4 of the pie:

Calories 267

Protein 20.5 g

Fat 4.25 g

Carbohydrates 34.25 g

2. Yoghurt ice cream

Ingredients:

Natural low-fat yogurt - 500 ml

Full-cream low-fat milk - 300 ml

Powdered milk - 3 tablespoons

Sugar - 4 tablespoons

Raspberries (you may use other berries, as you wish)

Some orange oil

Method of preparation:

1. Mix the sugar and the powdered milk in a saucepan, pour the full-cream milk, and boil over a slow fire.

2. Mix with the yogurt, pour the orange oil. The oil is used as a flavour additive, that's why you can miss this ingredient if you can't find it.

3. Mix it all together and put in the freezer. Don't forget to stir the recipe until it's completely frozen.

4. Mash the raspberries or other berries and use this mixture to decorate the ice cream before serving.

Nutrition value:

Raspberries contain such vitamins as A, B1, B2, B5, B6, C, E, and minerals like potassium, calcium, phosphorus, magnesium, etc. Raspberries preserve useful qualities even after heat treatment, therefore, raspberries do not lose their nutrients.

Yogurt contains a half of the recommended daily value of calcium, about 10-14 g of protein, it reduces the level of "bad" cholesterol and strengthens the immune system. A low-fat yogurt contains less 1 g of fats per 100 g of yogurt.

3. Vanilla protein pancakes

Ingredients:

Oatmeal - 1/4 cup

Liquid egg white - 1/2 cup

Vanilla protein - 1/8 cup

Chip coconut - 1/4 cup

Almond milk - 1/4 cup

Baking soda - 1/2 teaspoon

Method of preparation:

1. Mix all the ingredients together.

2. Grease the cake pan with oil.

3. Bring the heat to medium. Pour the batter into the hot cake pan. Slack the fire so the pancakes wouldn't burn.

4. Turn the pancakes when the surfaces get bubbles.

And boom - it's done!

Nutrition value (per one portion):

Calories 564

Fat 21 g

Carbohydrates 39 g

Protein 57 g

4. Cottage cheese pudding, or Cheesecake

Ingredients:

Acid curd (4%-5% fat, or degreased) - 700 g

Degreased milk - 100 ml

Semolina - 50 g

Eggs - 3 pieces

Baking powder - 1 sachet (meant for 500 g of flour)

Liquid sweetener for pastry - 5 ml

Butter for pan coating - 3-5 g

Liquid vanilla, flavouring agent - 1 parison

Method of preparation:

1. Pour the milk into the semolina and leave it for 7-10 minutes.

2. Mince the acid curd by mixer and make it smooth. You can use a blender, or use sugarless curds.

3. Beat the egg whites and yolks together into a rich light lather.

4. Add the 5 ml of sweetener and 1 sachet of baking powder to the curds, pour the wet semolina with milk, the liquid vanilla and whipped yolks. Mix it thoroughly. Add the whipped eggs and stir it carefully.

5. Grease the bottom of the baking dish with butter and powder with flour. You may use ramequins or one large baking dish).

6. Spread the mixture all over the baking dish (or into small ramekins).

7. Put it into heated oven (160-170 C) on the bottom shelf if using one large dish. Bake within an hour. After 20 minutes cover it with aluminium foil paper saving the top of the cake from burning. In case you use the muffin pans, heat the oven up to 150 C and bake the cake on the bottom shelf within half an hour.

Nutrition value (per cake):

Calories 990

Protein 100 g

Carbohydrates 98 g

Fat 40 g

5. Carrot-curd pudding with Philadelphia cheese

Ingredients:

Acid curd (4%-5% fat) - 600 g

Philadelphia cheese light - 100 g

Boiled carrot - 200 g

Eggs - 3 pieces

Baking powder - 1 sachet (meant for 500 g of flour)

Liquid sweetener for pastry - 5 ml

Butter for pan coating - 5 g

Method of preparation:

1. Mush the curd using blender or mixer.

2. Add the Philadelphia cheese, baking powder and sweetener to the curd.

3. Rub the carrots on a large or medium grater.

4. Froth the egg yolks and whites together.

5. Mix the curd and carrots and add the frothed eggs; mix it thoroughly.

6. Grease the pan with butter, and pour the mixture. You may use any pan, better to use a silicone deep square pan, filling it up to 2/3.

7. Put the pan on the bottom shelf of the oven previously heated to 160-170 C. After 10 minutes cover the pan with foil aluminium paper, it will help to preserve the top of the pudding from burning. After 30 minutes put the pan on the medium shelf, and after another 50 minutes remove the foil paper and leave the pudding to bake for 25 more minutes. Total baking should take not more than 75 minutes. In the end, take the pudding out of the oven and let it cool.

8. The best way to cool the pudding is putting it into the refrigerator for the night, it will be easier to cut it when cooled. After cooling turn the pudding upside down and cut into portions. It should look very attractive and appetizingly.

Nutrition value (per pudding):

Calories 981

Protein 91 g

Carbohydrates 38 g

Fat 49

6. Curd pudding with cherry

Ingredients:

Acid curd (4%-5% fat) - 700 g

Milk (0% low fat) - 100 ml

Semolina - 50 g

Eggs - 3 pieces

Baking powder - 1 sachet (meant for 500 g of flour)

Liquid sweetener for pastry - 5 ml

Cherry in own juice (fresh or frozen) - 175 g

Butter for pan coating - 3 - 5 g

Method of preparation:

1. Pour the milk into the semolina and leave it for 7-10 minutes.

2. Mince the acid curd by mixer and make it smooth. You can use a blender, or use sugarless curds.

3. Beat the egg whites and yolks together into a rich light lather.

4. Froth the egg whites until stiff.

5. Add 10 ml of sweetener, 1 sachet of baking powder, the pour the wet semolina with milk and frothed yolks to the

curds. Mix it thoroughly. Add the whipped eggs and stir it carefully.

6. Grease the pan with butter and strew it with semolina. Pour half of the batter, then cover it with cherries, after that pour the rest of the batter and put one more layer of cherries.

7. Put the pan into the heated oven (160-170 C) on the bottom shelf. After 10 minutes cover the pan with foil paper. After next 30 minutes remove the foil paper and more the pan onto the medium shelf; leave it for 20-25 minutes.

8. When ready, let the pudding cool for about 20 minutes, cover it with food wrap and put into the refrigerator.

Nutrition value for 1/4 of the pudding:

Calories 270

Protein 25.8

Carbohydrates 17.3

Fat 10.3

7. Protein pancakes with oat-flakes

Ingredients:

Curd (50% fat) - 50 g

Butter milk (kefir) - 50 ml

Oat-flakes - 25 g

Egg white - 1 piece (35 g)

Protein dry mixture - 10 g

Olive oil - 2 g

Method of preparation:

1. Mix the oat-flakes with butter milk and protein, leave it for about 10 minutes in order the oat-flakes become mushy.

2. After that mix all the ingredients together, pour the batter in the form of small pats on the previously heated crepe maker.

3. When ready powder the pancakes with powdered sugar or jam.

Oat-flakes contains saturated and desaturated fatty acids, food fiber, vitamins PP, E and minerals potassium, magnesium, calcium, phosphorus, sulfur, ferrum, iodine, copper and many others.

Nutrition value per portion:

Calories 242

Protein 23 g

Fat 7 g

Carbohydrates 19 g

8. Coconut pancakes

Ingredients:

Eggs - 1 piece

Egg whites - 2 piece

Coconut flour - 25 g

Yogurt or 10% fat sour cream - 30 g

Coconut oil (unpurified) - 5 g

Stevia - to taste

Salt - 1 pinch

Leaven - 1 teaspoon

Method of preparation:

1. Froth the eggs and mix them with stevia.

2. Add the yogurt and stir it thoroughly.

3. Warm the coconut oil (you can use a microwave), pour it into the eggs mixture and stir it thoroughly.

4. Add the leaven, salt and coconut flour.

5. Leave it for a few minutes so that the flour would absorb the liquids.

6. Heat the frying pan, oil it slightly with olive oil; the fire should be slow.

7. Bake the pancakes as usually, firstly on one side, then turning to other side. You can choose the size of pancakes at your taste.

You can add some pieces of bananas or raspberries to the baked pancakes as they are very rich in vitamins like A, B, C.

Coconut oil is rich in vitamins A, E, B1, B2, B3, K and C, and minerals ferrum, potassium, calcium, phosphorus, etc.

Nutrition value per portion:

Calories 343

Protein 21 g

Fat 15 g

Carbohydrates 4 g

Dietary fiber - 12 g

Sugar - 3 g

9. Carrot Zucchini Pie

Ingredients:

Baking dish 21-22 cm in diameter and 4.5 cm in height

Wholegrain wheat flour - 350 g

Carrots (gratings) - 360 g

Zucchini (gratings) - 180 g

Chicken eggs - 4 pieces

Olive oil - 60 g

Baking powder or soda - 1 full teaspoon

Ground cinnamon - 1 full teaspoon

Crystallized stevia - 2 tablespoons (or any other sweetener at your taste)

Light cream cheese for pan coating - 100 g (e.g., Philadelphia light)

Method of preparation:

1. Finely grate the carrots and zucchini.

2. Mix the wholegrain wheat flour with bakery powder and cinnamon; no salt needed.

3. Mix the eggs with olive oil and stevia; stir with grated vegetables.

4. Add the dry mixture of flour, baking soda and cinnamon. Mix it all thoroughly.

5. Put a bakery paper (21 cm in diameter) into the round shaped baking dish. Better to oil it slightly.

6. Carefully pour the batch into the dish, covering the whole bottom.

7. Bake the pie at 180 degrees C for 45-50 minutes.

8. Chill the pie and grease the surface with cream cheese Philadelphia light.

Carrots are very useful thanks to vitamins A, B, B3, B6, C, E, K and minerals like potassium, magnesium, calcium, phosphorus, sodium, copper, boron, fluorine, etc.

Zucchini is rich in potassium, dietary fiber, phosphorus and calcium, as well as in vitamins A and C.

Nutrition value per 1/4 of the pie:

Calories 540

Protein 17.5 g

Fat 19.8 g

Carbohydrates 74.2 g

Dietary fiber - 12.7 g

Sugar - 4.7 g

10. Coconut flour bread with zucchini, bananas and ginger

Ingredients:

Coconut (or almond) flour - 50 g

2.5% low fat milk - 50 ml

Chicken eggs - 3 pieces

Bananas - 85 g

Zucchini 85 g

Olive (or walnut) oil - 8 g

Ginger powder - 1 teaspoon (or rub the fresh ginger)

Baking powder (leaven or baking soda) - 1 teaspoon

A pinch of salt

Method of preparation:

1. Preheat the oven to 190 C.

2. Rub zucchini on a small grater and mash the banana with a fork; mix it all thoroughly.

3. Froth the eggs.

4. Stir the coconut flour with salt, baking powder and ginger powder, or add fresh ginger, and finely grated zucchini.

5. Add the flour mixture into the beaten-up eggs, stir it thoroughly; blend the mixture with zucchini and bananas and add 50 ml of milk. Stir it up and add the walnut oil or olive oil.

6. Put the baking paper into a square baking cup for bread and press it to the walls, place the dough into the cup.

7. Bake at 190 C for 40 minutes, until the tip and sides of the bread are lightly browned.

It's a fantastic bread!

Firstly, it contains a minimum of carbohydrates, secondly, there are a lot of proteins and fiber. It's like a cake, but without the butter.

Nutrition value per one bread (about 480 g):

Calories 62.7

Protein 32 g

Fat 27 g

Carbohydrates 37 g

Dietary fiber - 4 g

11. Coconut flour Muffins

Ingredients:

Sound eggs - 2 pieces

Egg whites - 3 (aprox.105 g)

Pure coconut flour - 50 g

Coconut oil Extra Virgin - 20 g (melted in microwave for 30 sec.)

Stevia or stevia powder (can be crystallized or liquid) - 1 tablespoon

Baking powder (or soda) - 1 full teaspoon

5% low fat curd - 100 g

Method of preparation:

1. Preheat the oven to 190 C.

2. Mix the baker powder, stevia and coconut flour.

3. Froth the 3 egg whites.

4. Froth the 2 eggs.

5. Add the curd, flour, stevia and baking powder to the 2 frothed eggs, stir it carefully.

6. Melt the oil in the microwave.

7. Stir together the mixture, the frothed egg whites and melted coconut oil. The dough should be crumbly because the coconut flour absorbs all the liquids thanks to the fiber.

8. Put the dough into baking cups for muffins (I spread equal parts of 66 grams in every shape. Gently press the dough to cups.

9. Bake in the oven on average temperature for about 25 minutes.

The coconut flour is rich in vitamins like A, C, E, D and B, and minerals like potassium salts, magnesium salts, iodine, cobalt and nickel. It contains lots of fibers and proteins. The consumption of coconut flour improves metabolism, stimulates digestion, has a positive effect on the skin and reduces the risk of thrombosis.

The portion contains 6 muffins.

Nutrition value per portion:

Calories 556

Protein 45 g

Fat 37 g

Carbohydrates 5 g

Dietary fiber - 30 g

12. Whole-wheat flour protein pancakes

Ingredients:

Fat-free milk - 720 ml

Eggs - 3 pieces

Butter - 50 g

Whole-wheat flour (course or fine ground) - 210 g

White flour - 50 g

Protein Optimum Nutrition (SAN, UNIVERSAL, TWINLAB - the one that you use) - 70 g

Salt at your taste

Powdered stevia - 1 teaspoon

Fresh boiling water - 120 ml

Method of preparation:

1. Firstly melt the butter in microwave and warm up the milk; froth the eggs.

2. Mix the wholegrain and white flour.

3. Mix the protein and stevia. That's the way the bio-protein should be like.

4. Mix the beaten eggs with milk and flour, add salt at your taste; add the protein with stevia into the dough and stir it

all carefully. Pour the melted butter and leave the mixture for 20-30 minutes at room temperature. Before you start baking pour 120 ml of boiling water into the dough.

5. Cook the pancake on a frying pan, but do not grease the pan. Pour one ladle full of batter and quickly spill it on the pan.

It's a perfect dish for breakfast. You can fill the pancakes with curd and pour some jam on top. Or, if for dinner, you can add some meat stuffing and sour cream.

Nutrition value per portion (2 pancakes):

Calories 246

Protein 17 g

Fat 7 g

Carbohydrates 28 g

13. Pancakes PROTEIN POW

Ingredients:

Oatmeal - 1/4 of a cup

Liquid egg whites - 1/2 cup

Vanilla protein - 1/8 cup

Chip coconut - 1/4 cup

Almond milk - 1/4 cup

Baking soda - 1/2 teaspoon

Method of preparation:

1. Stir all the ingredients together.

2. Spray the frying pan with oil and make the fire slow.

3. When the pan is red-hot, pour the batter in small portions, and make the fire slower to keep the pancakes from burning.

4. Turn the pancakes with a spatula when they get slightly brown.

If desired, you can pour some honey on top to the ready pancakes. Honey is rich in vitamin B (B1, B2, B6 and B9), as well as C, E, H, A, D; it contains minerals like potassium, phosphorus, magnesium, sodium, iodine, etc. Honey exhibits antibacterial, antifungal and antiviral action, improves the digestion, the condition of bones and teeth.

Almond milk contains potassium, calcium, magnesium, zinc, ferrum, selenium, dietary fiber; vitamins B2, B3, A, B-carotene,

Nutrition value per portion (a few pancakes):

Calories 564

Protein 57 g

Fat 21 g

Carbohydrates 39 g

14. Blueberry pancake with cinnamon

Ingredients:

Egg whites - 6 pieces

Oatmeal - 1/2 cup

Leaven - 1 teaspoon

Almond milk - 1/2 cup

A pinch of salt

Powdered artificial sweetener - 2 pinches

Blueberries - 1/4 cup

Applesauce - 1/2 cup

Cinnamon - 1 pinch

Method of preparation:

1. Put the egg whites, oatmeal, leaven, almond milk, salt and artificial sweetener into the blender, and mix them for 30 seconds at average speed.

2. Spray the frying pan with oil (sunflower oil or butter, at your taste), pour the batter and half of the blueberries. Cook it as usual pancakes - firstly on one side, then on another till browning.

When ready, serve with applesauce and cinnamon.

These pancakes are not only very delicious, but useful as well. Blueberries contain lots of dietary fibers, potassium, calcium, sodium, magnesium, ferrum, Vitamin C, pantothenic acid, glycoside, etc. Blueberries contributes to eyesight recovery, reduces the risk of glaucoma and cataract, improves the metabolism, and regulates the action of the bowels.

Nutrition value per portion (a few pancakes):

Calories 334

Protein 30 g

Fat 4 g

Carbohydrates 48 g

15. Kefir pancakes with vanilla and peanut butter

Ingredients:

Flour - 1 cup

Oatmeal - 1 cup

Leaven - 1.5 teaspoon

Salt - 0.5 teaspoon

Kefir - 2 cups

Low-fat milk - 1/2 cup

Vanilla extract - 1 teaspoon

Sound egg - 1 piece

Egg whites - 2 pieces

Peanut butter - 3 tablespoons

Fresh berries - 1 cup

Method of preparation:

1. Froth together one sound egg and 2 egg whites.

1. Mix the flour, oatmeal, leaven and salt in a large bowl, and the kefir, milk, vanilla extract and frothed eggs in another bowl. Combine the two mixtures and stir them together till smooth paste.

2. Heat the frying pan on a slow fire and spray it with oil. Pour the batter onto the pan using a large tablespoon; bake the pancakes for 1-2 minutes on one side and 1-2 minutes on another side till browning.

3. Melt the peanut butter in a microwave for 20-30 seconds, then grease the pancakes with it. Decorate the pancakes with berries.

Peanut butter has a high nutritional value, it consists of required digestible fats, vitamins A, E, B1, B2, B3, B4, B5, B8, B9), macro- and microelements potassium, magnesium, phosphorus, ferrum, zinc, iodine, cobalt, etc., monounsaturated oleic acid. Peanut butter strengthens the immune system, improves the cardiac function and blood vessels, improves the functioning of reproductive and nervous systems, and normalizes the hormonal balance and blood cholesterol levels.

Nutrition value per portion (a few pancakes):

Calories 584

Protein 28 g

Fat 15 g

Carbohydrates 81 g

16. Almond-saffron pancakes with cardamom

Ingredients:

Egg - 1 piece

Egg whites - 3 pieces

Almond milk - 180 ml

Vanilla extract - 1/2 teaspoon

Curd - 50-70 g

Tendrils of saffron - 5-7 pieces

Cardamom - 1/3 teaspoon

Almond flour - 1 tablespoon (about 13 g)

Coconut flour - 1 tablespoon

Psyllium (plantain's dietary fibers) - 2 tablespoons

Leaven - 1 teaspoon

Pure stevia - 1/3 teaspoon

Method of preparation:

1. Take the eggs out from refrigerator.

2. Heat the milk till hot state, add saffron and cardamom, and stir together.

3. Mix thoroughly all dry ingredients (almond flour, coconut flour, psyllium, leaven and pure stevia).

4. Whip the eggs with a wire whisk (one sound egg and three egg whites), add the milk with spices and other wet ingredients (curd, vanilla extract); stir carefully.

5. Mingle the two mixtures using a blender and leave the batter for about 20 minutes to rest.

6. Bake the pancakes on both sides till slight browning on a slow fire using no oil for the frying pan.

You can also prepare some side dish, for example using mango: finely chopped half of ripe mango, sugarless chip coconut, ground peanut and coconut sauce - mix all together thoroughly and decorate the pancakes.

Berries side dish: any berries at your taste, curd cream and tofu cream, ground almond, nibs mix in a blender to creamy state, serve with the pancakes.

Nutrition value per portion (5-6 pancakes):

Calories 240

Protein 22 g

Fat 12 g

Carbohydrates 16 g

Dietary fiber - 9 g

Sugar - 3 g

17. Oatmeal cake with whipped cream and nuts

Dry ingredients:

Oatmeal - 40 g (about 4 full tablespoons)

Blues - 1 tablespoon

Cinnamon - 1/3 teaspoon

Spices for recipes with pumpkin (cinnamon, cloves, nutmeg, ginger) - 1/4 teaspoon

Leaven - 1/4 teaspoon

Baking soda - 1/8 teaspoon

Wet ingredients:

Egg whites - 1 piece

Milk - 2 tablespoons

Sugarless applesauce - 1 tablespoon, or coconut/olive oil - 1 teaspoon

Vanilla extract - 1/2 teaspoon

Carrots - 1/2 medium pieces

Cream:

Ripe frozen banana - 1/4 pieces

Fat free curd - 100 g

Vanilla extract - 1/4 teaspoon

Banana extract - 1 drop (not necessary)

Natural sweetener at your taste

Honey - 1 tablespoon

Method of preparation:

1. Cook the carrot in a steamer, do it in advance to save time.

2. Preheat the oven and put inside a baking dish 7-8 cm in diameter with good nonstick coating.

3. Mix thoroughly all dry ingredients for the pie shell.

4. Mash the cooked carrot with a fork, divide in two portions - the small one for decoration.

5. Mix thoroughly all wet ingredients, and stir together both mixtures.

6. Pour the batter into the preheated baking dish and press it carefully with a spoon. Bake it for about 20-25 minutes at 180 C. Take care of it as all ovens work differently, don't let your cake burn. The pie shell should be neither dry nor wet, but with a slightly brown crust.

7. Whip all cream ingredients in a blender until smooth.

8. Take out the baked cake and let it cool in the baking dish for 7-10 minutes; slice it carefully

9. Share the cake in two parts. Lay out 1/3 of the cream on one part of the cake, put the other part on top and lay out the rest of the cream. You can powder some walnut on top if you like it and are not keeping any slimming diets.

Nutrition value for the whole cake:

Calories 336

Protein 30 g

Fat 6 g

Carbohydrates 42 g

Dietary fiber - 8 g

Sugar - 4 g

18. Biscuits with raisins and walnut

Ingredients:

Curd - 250 g

Oatmeal - 150 g

Bananas - 1 pieces

Raisins or dried apricots - 50 g

Walnut - 30 g

Poppy seeds, or chip coconut, or gingili

Method of preparation:

1. Mash together the curd and banana till smooth.

2. Add the oatmeal, raisins, ground walnut and knead the dough.

3. Leave the dough in the refrigerator for 1 hour.

4. When took out of the fridge, form small balls, roll in poppy seeds, or chip coconut, or gingili and turn the balls onto a baking tray previously covered with baking paper.

5. Preheat the oven to 180 C and cook the biscuits for 15 minutes.

Walnut core contains free amino acids, vitamin A, vitamins E, PP, K, C, B group, minerals like iodine, ferrum, zinc, phosphorus, etc. Walnuts reduce the risk of cardiovascular disease, reduce blood pressure, strengthen bone tissue, provide energy, activates the brain activity, and is used in the treatment of thyroid diseases.

Nutrition value for portion (150 g):

Calories 250.5

Protein 15 g

Fat 6.9 g

Carbohydrates 34.5 g

19. Coconut muffins

Ingredients:

Fat free curd - 300 g

Egg whites - 8 pieces

Sound eggs - 2 pieces

Powdered stevia - 4 full tablespoons

Coconut oil - 20 g

Olive oil - 20 g

Coconut flour - 100 g

Natural coconut extract - 3 drops

Leaven (double action) - 1.5 teaspoon

Method of preparation:

1. Mix together the sweetener, leaven and flour.

2. Work the egg whites into a rich lather; froth the two sound eggs till smooth.

3. Stir the frothed eggs and dry ingredients thoroughly.

4. Preheat the oven to 180 C.

5. Add the oil to the batter, then pour the coconut extract.

6. And place the dough into the cake pan; put it into the oven for about 30 minutes.

You can decorate the beaked muffins with some chocolate sauce: stir together 1 teaspoon of sugarless cocoa powder, 2 teaspoons of dry fat free peanut oil PB2, 1 teaspoon of stevia and some sugarless almond milk.

Nutrition per 2 muffins:

Calories 99

Protein 20 g

Fat 10 g

Carbohydrates 16 g

Dietary fiber - 4 g

20. Orange and yogurt protein cocktail

Ingredients:

Orange juice - 100 ml

Fat free yogurt - 100 ml

A handful of peeled orange pigs

Method of preparation:

1. Mix all the ingredients thoroughly in a blender till smooth.

Better to use a cooled juice, thus you'll have a refreshing cocktail.

Orange contains a lot of vitamin C, so it's useful to drink the cocktail in the morning to gain strength for the rest of the day.

Orange juice is very rich in vitamins A, B, C, K and E, and minerals like potassium, calcium, phosphorus, cuprum, ferrum, zinc, etc.

Nutrition:

Calories 198

Protein 23 g

Fat 1 g

Carbohydrates 40

21. Pomegranate protein cocktail

Ingredients:

Pomegranate juice - 170 ml

Egg whites - 75 g

Fat free yogurt - 180 g

Frozen berries mixture - 170 g

Method of preparation:

1. Mix all the ingredients thoroughly in a blender till smooth.

Better to use a cooled juice, thus you'll have a refreshing cocktail.

Pomegranate is very rich in vitamins PP, A, B1, B5, B6, C, E, and minerals calcium, magnesium, sodium, etc.

Red bilberries, blueberries and raspberries are a good combination for the given cocktail making it fresh and useful thanks to such vitamins as PP, C, E, A, B9, H, and minerals like calcium, magnesium, sodium, potassium, chloride, sulfur, phosphorus, etc.

Nutrition:

Calories 508

Protein 19 g

Fat 2 g

Carbohydrates 70

22. Red bilberries and almonds protein cocktail

Ingredients:

Red bilberries juice - 100 ml

Almonds - 2 full tablespoons

Fat free yogurt - 3 tablespoons

Method of preparation:

1. Mix all the ingredients thoroughly in a blender till smooth.

Red bilberries juice is very rich in vitamins PP, A, C, B9, E, and minerals like calcium, magnesium, sodium, sulfur, etc. Almonds will fill you with vitamins A, B1, B2, B6, B9, PP, E and C.

This cocktail will make your day!

Nutrition:

Calories 346

Protein 15

Fat 22 g

Carbohydrates 27 g

23. Fat free protein cocktail

Ingredients:

Low-fat milk - 340 ml

Fat free yogurt - 1 teacup

Flax seeds - 1 tablespoon

Strawberries - 0.5 teacup

Method of preparation:

1. Wash and clear the strawberries.

2. Mix together all ingredients - firstly milk with yogurt, then add the flax seeds and strawberries, stir till smooth.

Flax seeds are very useful thanks to vitamins B1, B3, high level of vitamin B9, K, PP, and minerals magnesium, potassium, phosphorus, cuprum, manganese. The dietary fiber of fax seeds help to waste removals and toxins; these seeds are often used for weighting loss.

Nutrition:

Calories 306

Protein 33 g

Fat 3 g

Carbohydrates 36 g

24. Protein cocktail with cocoa

Ingredients:

Curd - 300 g

Fat free milk - 200 ml

Water - 100-200 ml

Cocoa - 1 tablespoon

Method of preparation:

1. Using a blender or mixer stir together the water and milk, then add the curd, finally powder the cocoa; stir together till smooth.

You may add some walnuts which will increase the protein value and add a specific flavour.

Bon appetit!

Cocoa is useful for hart-vascular system as it reduces the platelet plug, has antioxidant properties, and influences the metabolism. Cocoa improves blood flow to the brain and reduces blood pressure. Regular consumption of cocoa promotes normal functioning of the skin and thereby substantially keeps it young.

Nutrition:

Calories 320

Protein 48 g

Fat 0 g

Carbohydrates 26

25. Kiwi and honey protein cocktail

Ingredients:

Almond milk - 300 ml

1.5 low fat kefir - 200 ml

Kiwi - 1 pieces

Honey - 1-2 tablespoons

Method of preparation:

1. Wash, clear and slice the kiwi to small pieces.

2. Slightly warm the honey.

3. Using a blender or mixer stir together the almond milk and kefir, add the sliced kiwi and honey; stir together till smooth.

Kiwi is rich in vitamins A, B9, C, and minerals potassium, calcium, chlorine, cuprum, boron, fluorine, etc.

Kiwi favorably effects the human immune system, strengthens the protection and regenerative functions, and increases the stress resistance of the organism.

Nutrition:

Calories 265

Protein 21 g

Fat 10 g

Carbohydrates 17 g

26. Protein sweet bar with peanut butter

Ingredients:

Peanut flour - 1/3 cup

Vanilla flavored protein - 1 full teaspoon

Almond milk - 100 ml

Almonds - 1 handful

Coconut flour - 2 tablespoons

Dark chocolate - 3-4 pieces

Method of preparation:

1. Mix all ingredients in a bowl except for chocolate and make it a dough. If the dough is too liquid or sticky, add some more coconut flour.

2. Shape rectangles from the dough.

3. Melt the chocolate using a water-bath, and dip the rectangular bars into the melted chocolate; take the bars out and put them into a silicone form or on foil paper.

Enjoy!

Peanut flour contains a lot of vitamin PP, B1, B5, B9, B4, and minerals ferrum, manganese, cuprum, selenium, zinc, etc. Peanuts improve the memory, concentration and nervous system, prevents diseases of the cardiovascular system, reduces the risk of heart attack, and helps to normalize blood pressure and metabolism.

Nutrition:

Calories 197

Protein 18 g

Carbohydrates 9 g

Fat 10 g

27. Caramel protein ice cream.

Ingredients:

Sugarless almond milk - 1 cup

Vanilla flavored protein - 1.5 scoop

Caramelized syrup - 2 tablespoons

Sea salt - 1 pinch

Method of preparation:

1. Mix the almond milk and powdered protein in a blender till smooth.

2. Pour the mixture into the cream freezer and turn it on.

3. After 10 minutes, add 1 tablespoon of caramelized syrup and stir together.

4. Mix it for about 10 minutes or till the ice cream gets hard enough.

5. Shift the ice cream to a dish and pour the rest of the caramelized syrup on top.

Bon appetit!

Caramel is rich in vitamins E and PP, and minerals potassium, magnesium, sodium, calcium, phosphorus and ferrum. Sweet caramel reduces the depression and enhances mood.

Nutrition:

Calories 235

Protein 35 g

Carbohydrates 8 g

Fat 8 g

28. Chocolate ice cream

Ingredients:

Chocolate flavored protein - 3 scoops

Fat free Greek yogurt (or any other filtered yogurt) - 0.5 cup

Sugarless vanilla almond milk - 1 cup

Almond oil - 1 teaspoon

Method of preparation:

1. Mix together all ingredients till smooth.

2. Pour the mixture into the cream freezer for about 20 minutes.

3. When ready, serve it in a dish adding some sliced bananas and caramelized syrup, or some instant Mocha coffee.

Chocolate contains anti-oxidant that is known for keeping youth, preventing development of malignant tumors and diseases of cardiovascular system. Chocolate is rich in minerals like calcium, magnesium, zinc, potassium, ferrum, and minerals PP, E and a little of B2.

Nutrition:

Calories 183

Protein 29 g

Carbohydrates 6 g

Fat 5 g

Dietary fiber 2 g

Sugar 2 g

29. Berries ice cream

Ingredients:

Fresh blueberries/raspberries/strawberries/dewberries - 1 cup

Pure water - 2 tablespoons

Vanilla extract - 1 teaspoon

Sugarless chocolate almond milk - 1 cup

Chocolate flavored protein - 0.5 cup

Almond oil - 1 tablespoon

Fat free Greek yogurt (or any other filtered yogurt) - 0.5 cup

Method of preparation:

1. Put the berries into a cooking pot and boil them on a slow fire until syrup (about 10-15 minutes).

2. Remove from fire and pour the vanilla extract; mix it and leave for a while.

3. Mix the milk, powdered protein, oil and yogurt thoroughly; add a half of the berries sauce.

4. Put the mixture into the cream freezer for about 20 minutes.

5. When ready serve the ice cream in a dish and decorate it with the rest of the berries sauce.

Enjoy!

Nutrition:

Calories 246

Protein 24 g

Carbohydrates 19 g

Fat 9 g

30. Lemon ice cream.

Ingredients:

Curd - 170 g
Milk - 100 ml
Egg whites - 2 pieces
Lemon flavored protein - 1 scoop
Lemon juice - 1 teaspoon
Lemon peel - 1 lemon

Method of preparation:

1. Forth the egg whites till smooth.

2. Add the milk, curd, powdered protein and lemon peel; stir thoroughly.

3. Put in the cream freezer for about 20 minutes.

4. Serve with a slice of lime and few leaves of mint.

Lemon is one of the most useful and vitamins rich fruits. This bitter fruit has strong antiseptic properties. The lemon juice is recommended against atherosclerosis, kidney stone diseases, metabolic disorders, fevers. Also this wonderful fruit increases appetite, improves digestion, helps reduce cholesterol levels in blood.

Lemon is very rich in vitamins, e.g. PP, A, B5, C, B9, E, and minerals calcium, potassium, phosphorus, magnesium, sodium, sulfur, cuprum, boron, fluorine, molybdenum, etc.

Nutrition:

Calories 353

Protein 33 g

Fat 22 g

Carbohydrates 12 g

31. Rum ice cream

Ingredients:

Powdered protein - 1 scoop

Curd - 120 g

Low fat milk - 150 ml

Egg whites - 2 pieces

Sweetener - to taste (or 1 teaspoon of honey)

Raisins - 10 g

Strawberry jam - 20 g

Method of preparation:

1. Presoak the raisins in the rum.

2. Work the egg whites into a rich lather; add the powdered protein, sweetener (or honey), curd and milk, and stir together thoroughly.

3. Put the mixture into the cream freezer for about 30-40 minutes. 10 minutes before the ice cream is ready add the raisins and strawberry jam to the freezer.

Raisins are very rich in potassium, phosphorus, sodium, calcium and magnesium, vitamins PP, B1, B2. Raisins are recommended to use against diseases such as fever, anemia, digestive system and kidneys diseases.

Nutrition:

Calories 109 g

Protein 16 g

Carbohydrates 7 g

Fat 2 g

32. Fat free protein cocktail

Ingredients:

Soft fat free yogurt - 125 g

Fat free milk - 125 ml

Fast-frozen strawberry - 50 g

Method of preparation:

1. Mix all ingredients in a blender till smooth.

2. You can add a teaspoon of honey if you want the cocktail to be sweeter.

Nutrition:

Calories 149

Protein 25 g

Fat 1 g

Carbohydrates 11 g

33. Chocolate orange protein bread

Ingredients:

Chocolate flavored protein - 3 scoops

Almond (or oatmeal) flour - 1 cup

Egg - 2 pieces

Orange - 2 pieces

Baking powder / leaven - 1 teaspoon

Fat free yogurt - 1 tablespoon

Melted bitter chocolate - 2 tablespoons

Method of preparation:

1. Mix thoroughly the liquid ingredients: eggs, orange, yogurt and melted chocolate.

2. Mix the dry ingredients; stir the two mixtures.

3. Preheat the oven to 160 C.

4. Pour the batter into the baking dish (square, rectangular or round) and put into the oven for 45 minutes.

You can powder the bread with some powdered sugar. It's a perfect supplement to breakfast or tea.

Nutrition:

Calories 190

Protein 16 g

Fat 5 g

Carbohydrates 22 g

34. Strawberry protein cheesecake bar

Ingredients:

For the basic dough:

Sweet bar with the taste of strawberry cheesecake - 1 piece

Peanut butter - 2 tablespoons

Nuts - 0.5 cup (almonds, walnuts, peanut, etc)

For the filling:

Low fat yogurt - 500 g

Vanilla protein - 0.5 cup

Egg whites - 1 cup

Fresh sliced strawberry - 0.5 cup (or any other berries you prefer)

Method of preparation:

1. Heat the sweet bar in a microwave for 10-15 minutes till soft; stir it together with ingredients for the basic dough till hard batter.

2. Knead the dough in a shape so it could cover the bottom and put it into the baking dish.

3. Prepare the filling by mixing the yogurt, vanilla protein and egg whites.

4. Pour the filling onto the basic dough and cover it with a layer of strawberry jam.

5. Bake the cake for about 40-50 minutes at 160 C till it gets a little hard on sides and remains soft inside and in the middle. Do not overbake the cake, it should be creamy, it will get harder after cooling.

6. Leave the cake in the refrigerator for 2 hours.

7. Voila! You can serve the cheese cake, don't forget to decorate the cheesecake with fresh berries and prepare some tea and...Bon appetit!

Nutrition per one slice/portion:

Calories 170

Protein 17 g

Carbohydrates 9 g

Fat 8 g

35. Chocolate protein bar

Ingredients:

Sugarless muesli - 35 g

Vanilla casein - 35 g

Chocolate casein - 25 g

Cocoa powder - 2 tablespoons

Dietary fiber - 10 g

Walnuts - 15 g

Oatmeal flour - 70 g

Fat free yogurt - 120 g

Cinnamon - 1 teaspoon

80% chocolate - 20 g

Liquid sweetener - few drops (you can use any other sweetener you prefer)

Method of preparation:

1. Mix all ingredients together till smooth and make the sweet bars by sculpturing the dough into square slices.

2. Melt the chocolate and spread it on the bars; put the bars into the refrigerator.

You can powder some ground nuts on top if wanted.

Nutrition:

Calories 274

Protein 22 g

Carbohydrates 24 g

Fat 9 g

36. Peanut protein bar

Ingredients:

Fat free peanut flour - 1/3 cup

Vanilla flavored protein - 1/3 cup

Coconut or almond milk - 1/4 cup

Almonds - 1/3 cup

Coconut flour - 2 tablespoons

Bitter chocolate 80% - 3-4 pieces

Method of preparation:

1. Mix all ingredients, except chocolate, in a bowl till dough to be easy to knead by hands. If it's too liquid or sticky add more coconut flour.

2. Form the dough into rectangles from.

3. Melt the chocolate using a water bath and dip the bars in the chocolate; put them on a silicon tray covered with foil paper - it will keep the chocolate from running out.

What a wonderful dessert for a tea break at work or among friends!

Nutrition:

Calories 197

Protein 18 g

Carbohydrates 9 g

Fat 10 g

37. French protein bar

Ingredients:

Vanilla protein - 1/4 cup

Coconut flakes - 1/4 cup

Liquid sweetener / honey - 1 tablespoon

Almond or coconut milk - 1/8 cup

Almonds - 3/8 cup

Dark chocolate - 3-4 pieces

Method of preparation:

1. Using a spoon or a spatula mix all ingredients in a bowl till dough. If the mixture is too sticky, add some more almonds.

2. Divide the dough into 4 balls and shape them into rectangles.

3. When the bars are patted, melt the chocolate via a water bath.

4. Place the bars in the melted chocolate so that they are fully covered.

5. Take out the bars, put them on a foil paper, then replace the bars into the refrigerator for 1-2 hours.

Nutrition per 2 bars:

Calories 382

Protein 22 g

Carbohydrates 7 g

Fat 14 g

38. Coffee protein muffins

Ingredients:

Egg - 2 pieces

Fat free curd - 150 g

Oat bran - 2 tablespoons

Chocolate protein - 2 scoops

Leaven / baking powder - 1 sachet

Instant coffee - 2 teaspoons

Vanilla syrup - 2 tablespoons

Sweetener / honey - at your taste

Method of preparation:

1. Froth the eggs with the curd.

2. Step by step add the rest of ingredients and stir it all together.

3. Preheat the oven to 170 C.

4. Put the mixture into muffin pans and bake at 170 C for half an hour.

Oat flakes are used for cleansing the gastrointestinal tract, for removing toxins and wastes, for detoxification of organism. Oat flakes reduce the level of cholesterol, strengthens the immune system, are very useful for heart-vascular system and are used against pancreatic diabetes.

Oat flakes contain many vitamins like B1, B5, B9, E, K, gossypine, and minerals such as phosphorus, potassium, magnesium, calcium, selenium, cuprum, ferrum, zinc, etc.

Nutrition per 100 g:

Calories 177

Protein 20 g

Carbohydrates 10 g

Fat 4 g

39. Banana protein bar

Ingredients:

Oatmeal - 1 cup

Banana flavored protein - 5 tablespoons

Fat free powdered milk - 1/2 cup

Fat free cream cheese - 1/4 cup

Egg whites - 2 pieces

Banana - 1 piece

Blueberry - 1 cup

Water - 1/4 cup

Rape oil for pan coating - 3 teaspoons

Method of preparation:

1. Preheat the oven to 160 C.

2. Mix the oatmeal, powdered protein and powdered milk together.

3. In a separate bowl mix the cream cheese, egg whites, banana, blueberries, water and oil.

4. Oil the baking pan.

5. Mix all ingredients together thoroughly with a mixer.

6. Pour the mixture into a square baking pan, put the pan into the oven and bake the bars for 25-30 minutes.

Totally you'll have about delicious and nutritious 7 bars.

Nutrition per bar:

Calories 180

Protein 18 g

Carbohydrates 20 g

Fat 3 g

40. Vanilla orange protein bar

Ingredients:

Oatmeal - 2 cups

Vanilla or chocolate flavored protein - 4 tablespoons

Fat free powdered milk - 1 cup

Maple syrup - 1 cup

Natural orange juice - 1/4 cup

Vanillin - 1 teaspoon

Egg whites - 2pieces

Rape oil for pan coating - 3 teaspoons

Method of preparation:

1. Preheat the oven to 160 C.

2. Mix the oatmeal, protein and powdered milk in a bowl.

3. In another bowl mix the rest of ingredients.

4. Grease the square baking pan with rape oil.

5. Using a mixer, mix together all ingredients.

6. Pour the batter into the baking pan, put into the oven and bake until brown, about 20-30 minutes.

Finally you'll have about 9 delicious bars.

Nutrition per bar:

Calories 195

Protein 15 g

Carbohydrates 27 g

Fat 3 g

41. "Power-Punch" protein bar

Ingredients:

Oatmeal - 1/2 cup

Wheat flour or oat flakes - 1/2 cup

Vanilla flavored protein - 6 tablespoons

Fat free powdered milk - 1 cup

Flax seeds - 2 tablespoons

Sunflower seeds - 2 tablespoons

Nuts - 1/4 cup

Dry fruits - 1/4 cup

Peanut butter - 1/3 cup

Vanillin - 2 teaspoons

Water - 1/2 cup

Method of preparation:

1. Mix in a bowl the oatmeal, oat flakes, protein, powdered milk, seeds, nuts and dry fruits.

2. Then add the peanut butter, vanillin and water, and stir thoroughly.

3. Pour the batter in an appropriate dish and place it into the refrigerator for about an hour till hard.

Nutrition per bar:

Calories 304

Protein 26 g

Carbohydrates 23 g

Fat 12 g

42. Coconut protein shake

Ingredients:

Almond milk - 300 ml

Curd - 300 g

Cocoa - 2-3 tablespoons

Walnut - 10 pieces

Chip coconut - 1 pinch

Method of preparation:

1. Put all ingredients in the blinder and stir it thoroughly for about 7-10 minutes.

Walnuts are very rich in vitamins PP, A, B1, B2, B5, B6, B9, C, E, K, and minerals phosphorus, potassium, calcium, magnesium, sulfur, zinc, cuprum, fluorine, iodine, and many others.

Nutrition:

Calories 730

Protein 62.5 g

Carbohydrates 21 g

Fat 36.5 g

43. Banana protein shake

Ingredients:

Fat free milk - 1 cup

Whey protein - 1 tablespoon

Banana - 1 piece

Nut oil - 1 tablespoon

Method of preparation:

1. Put all ingredients into the blender and mix it thoroughly.

For this cocktail you can also use cocoa oil with no sweetener and flavoring agents, or olive oil.

Nutrition:

Calories 461

Protein 37 g

Carbohydrates 46 g

Fat 16 g

44. Homemade protein shake

Ingredients:

Chocolate whey protein - 1 tablespoon

Fat free milk - 1 cup

Ground almond - 1/2 cup

Ground chocolate bar - 1/2 piece

Method of preparation:

1. Mix the protein and milk in the blender.

2. Then powder the ground almonds and ground bar on top.

Nutrition:

Calories 457

Protein 39 g

Carbohydrates 41 g

Fat 17 g

Dietary fiber 8 g

45. Peach protein drink

Ingredients:

Vanilla whey protein - 1 tablespoon

Water - 1 cup

Instant oatmeal - 1 sachet

Canned peaches - 1/2 can

Method of preparation:

1. Mix all ingredients in a blender till smooth.

Oatmeal is very rich in dietary fiber. If you don't like oatmeal, use cornflakes.

Nutrition:

Calories 306

Protein 24 g

Carbohydrates 49 g

Fat 2 g

Dietary fiber 2 g

46. Homemade orange protein mix

Ingredients:

Vanilla whey flavored protein - 1 tablespoon

Orange juice - 1 cup

Fat free vanilla yogurt - 1/2 cup

Method of preparation:

1. Mix all ingredients in a blender.

Orange is rich in vitamin C, B9, PP, E, A, and minerals potassium, phosphorus, calcium, cuprum, iodine, boron, etc.

Nutrition:

Calories 280

Protein 27 g

Carbohydrates 43 g

Fat 1 g

Dietary fiber 2 g

47. Homemade vanilla protein mix

Ingredients:

Vanilla casein - 1 tablespoon

Vanilla whey protein - 1 tablespoon

Vanilla milk - 1/2 cup

Vanilla fat free yogurt - 1/2 cup

Method of preparation:

1. Stir in a bowl the protein and yogurt till smooth.

2. Pour the milk in a large glass and add the mixture of protein and yogurt, mix it carefully.

There is no need to use a blender as the protein was already mixed with yogurt.

Nutrition:

Calories 443

Protein 48 g

Carbohydrates 61 g

Fat 1 g

48. Kiwi and honey protein drink

Ingredients:

Almond milk - 300 ml

1.5 % low fat kefir - 200 ml

Kiwi - 1 piece

Honey - 1-2 tablespoons

Method of preparation:

1. Mix all ingredients till smooth using a blender.

Kiwi is rich in vitamins A, B9, C, PP, B6, and minerals potassium, calcium, magnesium, phosphorus, chlorine, sulfur, iodine, cuprum, fluorine, boron, aluminum, etc.

Nutrition:

Calories 265

Protein 21 g

Carbohydrates 17 g

Fat 10 g

49. Raspberry protein shake

Ingredients:

Milk - 200 ml

1.5 % low fat natural sugarless yogurt - 200 ml

Raspberry - 100 g (fresh or frozen)

Method of preparation:

1. Mince the raspberries.

2. In a blender mix the milk and yogurt, then add the minced raspberries.

Use some honey if you want your cocktail to be sweeter.

Raspberries are rich in vitamins A, B9, H, C, PP, E, B5, and minerals potassium, calcium, magnesium, sodium, phosphorus, chlorine, etc.

Raspberries are used to reduce the fever when sick, stop the bleeding and reduce the toxins.

Nutrition:

Calories 224

Protein 17 g

Carbohydrates 24 g

Fat 6 g

50. Mandarin protein shake

Ingredients:

Milk - 400 ml

1.5 % low fat kefir - 125 ml

Mandarin - 2 pieces

Flax oil - 1 teaspoon

Method of preparation:

1. Slice the mandarins.

2. Mix in a blender the milk, kefir and oil, add the sliced mandarins.

Mandarins are rich in vitamins A, D, K, C, PP, and minerals potassium, calcium, magnesium, sodium and phosphorus.

Mandarins are good in allaying thirst and saturates the organism with the needed amount of ascorbic acid; it partially reduces fever when sick.

Nutrition:

Calories 280

Protein 21.5 g

Carbohydrates 18 g

Fat 11.5 g

Other Great Titles by This Author

www.ingramcontent.com/pod-product-compliance
Lightning Source LLC
Chambersburg PA
CBHW071745080526
44588CB00013B/2154